Plank Road Explorer

by Henry Marvin

Webbs Mills, New York
February 19, 1873 - February 17, 1874

transcribed by Diane Janowski

New York History Review Press
Elmira, New York

Plank Road Explorer
by Henry Marvin
transcribed by Diane Janowski
photographs by Allen C. Smith
Copyright © 2011 New York History Review Press

Published by New York History Review Press
Elmira, New York

Notice of Rights. All rights reserved. No part of this book may be reproduced or transmitted in any form by any means, electronic, mechanical, photocopying, recording or otherwise, without the prior written permission of the author. For more information on getting permission for reprints and excerpts, contact us through our website.
www.NewYorkHistoryReview.com

For the latest on New York History Review, please visit
www.NewYorkHistoryReview.com

ISBN: 978-0-9838487-0-7

First Edition

Printed in the United States of America

The boy stood on the burning deck
Eating peanuts by the peck;
The flames that led the battle
Just singed his hair a little.

a variation of a poem by
Felicia Dorothea Hemans

written in the back of Henry's diary

Table of Contents

Foreward..8
Maps of Webbs Mills...10, 11
People in the Diary...12
Plank Road Explorer..17
Afterward...75
Marvin Family History..76
Bibliography..78

Foreword

In our *Learning from History* series of Upstate New York diaries, accounts of young people's lives on the farm, or in the home, help us to understand their thoughts and experiences. Each narrative offers a unique perspective on young peoples' lives in rural New York, and serves as an important primary resource in the study of American history.

Plank Road Explorer is the journal of 18-year-old Henry Marvin of Webbs Mills, New York - seven miles southwest of Elmira, New York. This book uses the name "Webbs Mills" as Henry did. Official documents and maps also frequently call it "Webb Mills" or "Webbs Mill."

Henry was born on February 14, 1855 in Webbs Mills, the son and youngest child of Seth and Susan Marvin. He had an older brother Lyme and older sister Het that lived nearby. He had several other siblings who lived elsewhere and are not mentioned in the diary.

Beginning on February 19, 1873, Henry recorded the events of his life in a small 3¼ x 4¾ inch pocket diary with one entry to the page in very nice handwriting. Henry's notations were confined to the spaces allotted and written in pencil. His handwriting is mostly legible, except for a few names or places that cannot be deciphered. Henry's spelling is left as he spelled it. Clarifications have been added in brackets. The photographed pages from his diary are actual size.

Henry had reddish-brown hair. He was eighteen years old and lived with his parents. He seemed very happy in his life – he enjoyed his family, friends, hunting, and fishing. His family's home was on Bird Creek Road and their farm bordered the "Plank Road" - an early toll road in Chemung County. Henry did much work on the farm and also helped his neighbors. He worked long hours to maintain the Plank Road and its bridge.

Plank Road Explorer invites us into the daily life of a New York young man through his own words and experiences. We hear Henry's voice as he shares his joys, sorrows, enthusiasm, and fragility of life in a rural farming community.

The Eleanor Barnes Library acquired Henry Marvin's diary in 2010. So far as is known, this transcription is its first published version. All of the photographs are by Allen C. Smith.

Diane Janowski, Publisher

Henry's family home still exists on Bird Creek Road in Webbs Mills.

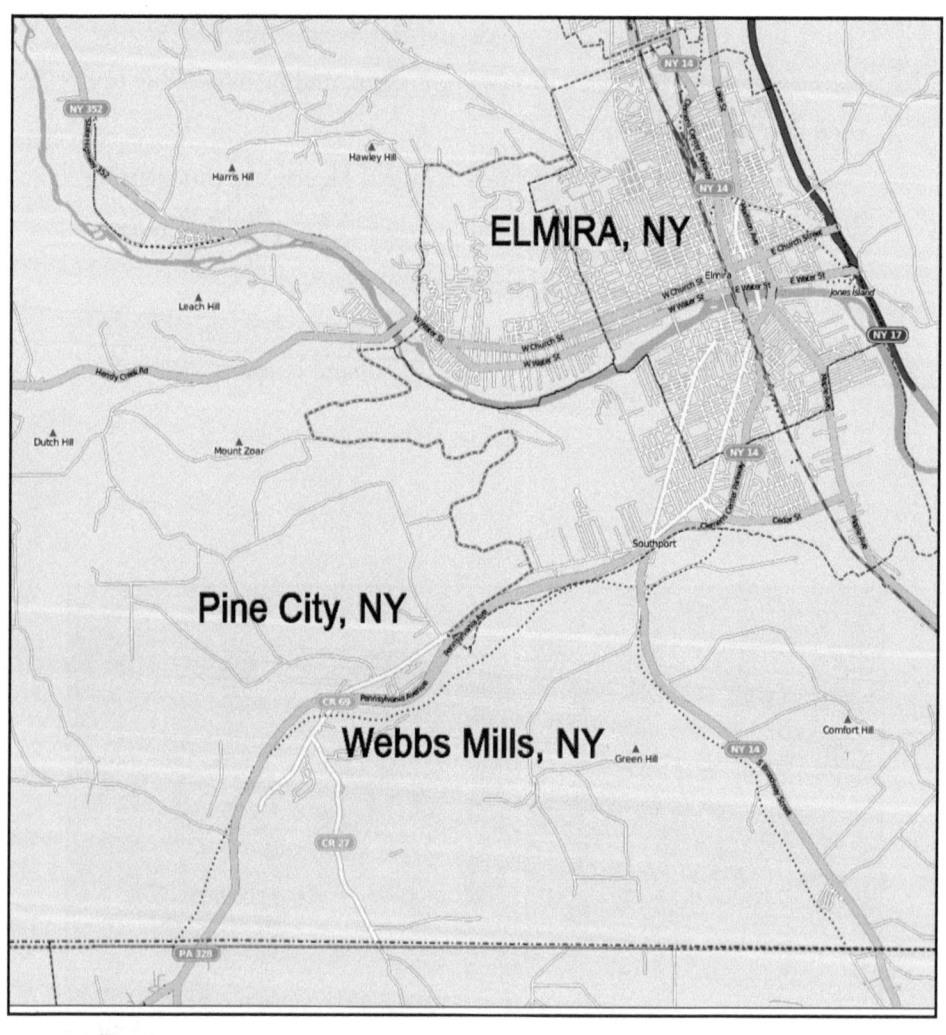

Webbs Mills is about seven miles south-west of Elmira, New York.

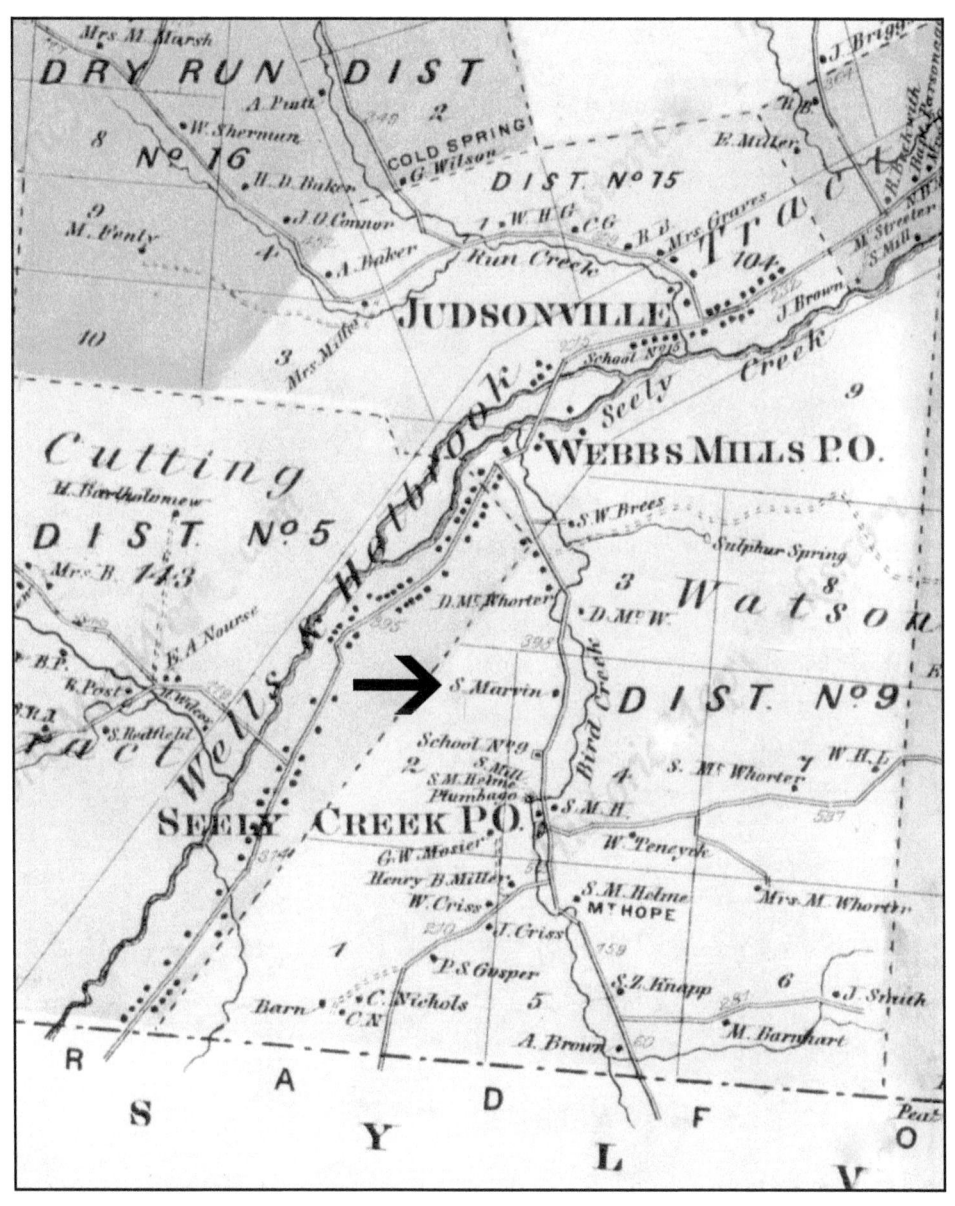

Henry Marvin lived at his parents house on Bird Creek Road in Webbs Mills, New York.

People in the Diary
Henry's family

Seth – father, age 63 farmer
Jane – mother, age 32
Het - probably his sister Helen age 21
Lyme – brother Lyman - farmer age 30, wife Jane or Mary Jane, age 23, and son Alex age 2 - lived in Elmira[?]
Aunt Julia Beckwith - lived in Pine City
Ed - brother [sometimes Edward, sometimes Edwin] & wife Mary

Friends and Relations

Charley Baker - age 21 - lived next to Aunt Julia
Lafe Bailey - lived in Millport, New York
Barker
Miny [Minnie?] Barker - age 17 - lived next to Aunt Julia
Minor Barnhart - "Old Barnhart" age 61 lived two doors away
John & Abba Beckwith
Dan Beckwith
Jane Bentley
Bertha
William Brace
Bradbury [Thomas Bradbury]- age 66, farmer, lived nearby
Thomas Bradbury - age 13, son of Thomas
Mr. Breese
Abe Breese
Nate Brewer
Will Brewer
Jim Brink
James Carman
Ida Coe
Mrs. Cole
Will Colegrove

Susan Colegrove
Covel/Covell
Jessie Criss - age 28, farmer, lived 3 doors away
U.B. Dann
Dan
Dave - David McWhorter
Early
Ed Barnhart, age 21, lived two houses away
Elake
Filander
O.H. Fitch
John and Lib Flynn
Frank
Mr. Gosper
Daniel Gray
Max Hait [Haight]
Nat Hait [Haight]
Silw - [Sylvester?] Hall
Mrs. Hammond
John Hathorn
Will Helme
Mrs. Helme
Frank Hill
Miss Hill
Net Humel [Hummel] or Nettie Hurnel?
George Huntley - farmer age 59 lived in Southport
Miss Huntley
Bob Jenkins
Harris Jenkins
John
John Kile
Mathis Knapp
Dr. Leonard
Lewis Wells - tanner, age 37 - lived in Webbs Mills

Lib, sometimes Libbie - lived with Aunt Julia
Het Lockwood - [Esther? age 28, lived nearby]
Harry Lyons
Mary Harvey Lyons
Dan Mack - age 28, lived in Elmira
David M
Sarah Manroe - Henry's date at a dance
Ed and Mary Mapes
Mart
Mary
Bill McCann
McCann
Sarah McC
Miles McWhorter - age 16, lived next door
Sarah McWhorter - age 17, lived nearby
Ed McConnell
Sam McWhorter - age 18 lived next door
Dave McWhorter - age 47, father of Sam
Wilson Mashel [Michael] - carpenter, age 43 - lived in Elmira
Mily - sometimes Millie
Lifa Miller
Fet [Fenton?] Miller - age 13, lived nearby
Henry Miller - age 43, farmer, lived next door
Judd Miller
Sam Miller - age 53, farmer , lived nearby
Gusta [Augusta] Misner - age 20
George Mosher - age 73, farmer, lived two doors away
Abbie Nichols - maybe Albert - age 15, lived nearby
Carrie Nichols - age 13, lived nearby
Hiram Pederick [Pedrick]
Petey/Peter
Charley Pierce - age 30, teamster
Mary Piper
Hiram Redstick [Redfield?]
John and Albert Robins /Robbins [Albert was a physician, age 28

lived in Southport]
Emma Robbins
Mose Scofield
Ed Scofield
Schofield
Mr. Snell
Burr Soaper
Frank Stofford/Stafford
Tim Sullivan
Susan - Susie
Tony
Pa Tanner
Sherman Tanner
Bill Teneyck [William Tenike] age 48, carpenter, lived nearby
George Teneyck - age 16, son of Bill
John Teneyck
Tim
Tom & Bertha
Chris John [Christian] Watkins
Mose Webb
Mrs. Wood
Ed and Steve Weaver
Lewis Wells
Welles/Wells
Lanson [?] White
Mr. White
Mr. Wilder
H. S. Wylie - teacher

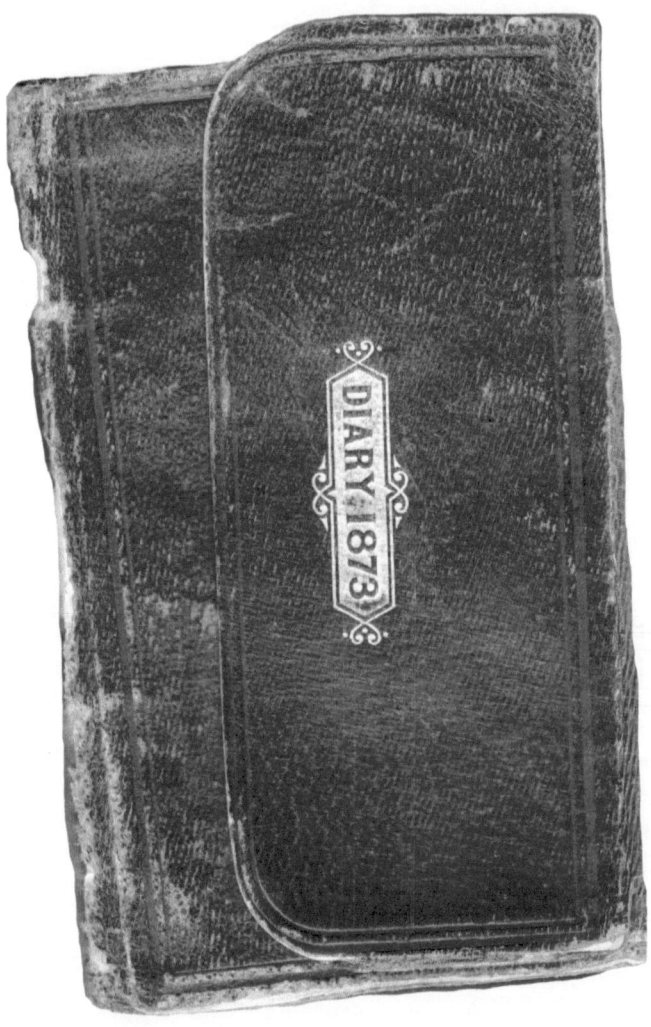

Henry's diary in its current condition.
Courtesy of the Eleanor Barnes Library, Elmira, New York.

Henry Marvin
Webbs Mills
Chemung County, New York
February 19, 1873 - February 17, 1874

February, Wednesday 19, 1873

I had a present of this book tonite. Father & Mother went to town [Elmira, New York] today. I went to school most all day. This afternoon I had a call to come home and work. Lyme come here this morning & stayed most all day. The snow is all most gone. Hiram Pederick's [Pedrick] child died on the 18th. He lost one on the 15th. Ed was here last week & Mary come after him to work on the street cars.

February, Thursday 20, 1873

I stayed at home all day & at nite I went to writing school. Gusta Misner was here. She stayed here till Saturday. Lyme & Jane was here. Father & Mother went to Mapes' to eat chickens.

February, Friday 21, 1873

I stayed at home all day. The snow is about six inches deep.

February, Saturday 22, 1873

I sawed wood in the forenoon & in the afternoon I went to the mill. We took a load of wood to Barker.

February, Sunday 23, 1873

I stayed at home all day. Gusta [Augusta] Misner was there. There is nothing going on.

February, Monday 24, 1873

I stayed at home all day.

February, Tuesday 25, 1873

I stayed at home all day.

February, Wednesday 26, 1873
I stayed at home all day & at nite I went down to Pine Woods with Sam & then we come home & went down to meeting. Sam has got peas.

February, Thursday 27, 1873
I stayed at home all day.

February, Friday 28, 1873
I took a load of wood up to Henry Miller's & at nite Pa went down to the store & we throwed pennies for the Candy. I got struck.

March, Saturday 1, 1873
I stayed at home all day. Lyme & Frank was here. Lyme & Father went to town. He stayed here all nite.

March, Sunday 2, 1873
I stayed at home most all day. --- up to Teneycks and got the broad az [adz or axe]. John & --- & son & Early & Frank & Lyme & Jane & Alex & Mrs. Hammond & Filandler & Sam McWhorter & John Hathorn & his father was here & George Mosher. Het has gone up to George Huntley.

March, Monday 3, 1873
I stayed at home all day. Lyme & Jane & Alex was here & stayed all nite. It is colder than the Devil. The snow is about 6 inches deep.

March, Tuesday 4, 1873
I stayed at home all day and at nite I went to Meeting & to the store & to writing school. It is colder than the Devil.

March, Wednesday 5, 1873
I stayed at home all day & at nite I went up to Singing School at the school house.
Where throughout History [name of a book?]
Lafe Baley. [Lafayette Bailey lived in Millport, NY]

There was a store located in this Webbs Mills vicinity in 1873. Photograph taken in summer 2011.

March, Thursday 6, 1873
I went to Meeting down to the Meeting house. I stayed at home all day.

March, Friday 7, 1873
I stayed at home all day. Then to meeting at nite.

March, Saturday 8, 1873
I helped draw wood all day & at nite I went to the Burg. Lina was here & stayed all nite.

March, Sunday 9, 1873
I went up to Tim's & we went a-cooning & then we went around through the woods home. John & Ab [John & Abba Beckwith] & Sam & Early & Silw [Sylvester?] Hall was here.

March, Monday 10, 1873
I stayed at home all day.

MARCH   THURSDAY, 13   1873.

I stayed at Home all day and at nite I went up to the School House to an Exabition we had a first rate one
Lime was here and Stayed all nite

MARCH   FRIDAY, 14   1873.

I stayed at home to day to day was the last day of School the teacher gave us all a Card with his name

H S Wylie

Father got a new wagon

March, Tuesday 11, 1873
I stayed at home all day & at nite I went to the Burg & got the paper. Lyme was here & stayed all nite.

March, Wednesday 12, 1873
I stayed at home all day. Lyme was here & stayed all nite.

March, Thursday 13, 1873
I stayed at home all day and at nite I went up to the school house to an Exabition. We had a first rate one. Lyme was here and stayed all nite.

March, Friday 14, 1873
I stayed at home all day today. Was the last day of school. The teacher gave us all a card with his name
H. S. Wylie.
Father got a new wagon.

March, Saturday 15, 1873
I stayed at home in the forenoon and thrashed oats and in the afternoon I went up to the Mill and got a load of wood. Lyme was here and stayed all nite.

March, Sunday 16, 1873
I went up to Lyme's a-cooning and we had three in one hole. I tried to dig out but I could not get them. Lyme and Jane and Alex was here and stayed all nite.

March, Monday 17, 1873
I thrashed oats all day and at nite I went to the Post office and up to the store. Lyme and Jane and Alex was here and stayed all nite.

March, Tuesday 18, 1873
I stayed at home all day and trimmed apple trees. It snowed in the afternoon. Lyme and Jane and Alex was here and stayed all nite.

March, Wednesday 19, 1873

I stayed at home all day. Father went to Tanner's. There was a fox chase down to Pine Woods. Lyme was here and stayed all nite. Frank was here.

March, Thursday 20, 1873

I went down to the store and up to the Vendue to Mrs. Wood's. Tim Sullivan was here and eat dinner. Lyme was here and went to the Vendue too. It snowed all day. Father went to town.

March, Friday 21, 1873

I stayed at home all day. The snow is about 8 inches deep and it is a-snowing yet.

March, Saturday 22, 1873

I stayed at home all day and at nite I went down to the Burg.

March, Sunday 23, 1873

I stayed at home all day. John and Lib and Sam and Early was here. Tim was here for the first time.

March, Monday 24, 1873

I stayed at home all day and trimmed apple trees. Lafe Bailey got hurt – the wagon tipped over with him and hurt his head. I went down to the Burg at nite.

March, Tuesday 25, 1873

I stayed at home all day. It rained in the afternoon. McCann beat a pair of Covel's horses up here to keep today. --- went to town today.

March, Wednesday 26, 1873

I stayed at home all day. John and Albert Robins was here and stayed all day. It snowed all day. The snow is about 10 inches deep and is a-snowing yet.

Henry mentions the "Big Bridge." This is its contemporary version. Photograph taken in summer 2011.

The "Burg" refers to downtown Webbs Mills which had two stores, two mills, a cigar factory, a boot and watch store, a cabinet shop, a wagon shop, and Henry's Methodist church. This building was one of the mills. Photograph taken in summer 2011.

"Going to town" meant going to Elmira - about seven miles northeast of Webbs Mills. Elmira had a population of 15,863 in 1870 with many stores and shops from which to choose. This photograph is looking north up Lake Street by W. J. Moulton.

March, Thursday 27, 1873
I stayed at home all day. John come here and him and father went to town and Het come home with them. Ed McConnell and his wife and Susie come over here. Ed come over here to work.

March, Friday 28, 1873
I stayed at home in the forenoon and in the afternoon I went down to the Burg and to Pine Woods and to Susie's. Lyme and Jane and Alex and M---[census lists a "May"] Sweet and Judd and Henry Miller was here today.

March, Saturday 29, 1873
I stayed at home all day. It rained and snowed all day. The creek is so high that they had to take up all of the planks off the Bridge.

March, Sunday 30, 1873
I went up Mud Hill. The bridge was gone and we come back and went up to the state line and we went up to the Rathbun House [in Elmira].

March, Monday 31, 1873
I worked on the road and at nite I went up to the Burg. Lyme and Alex and Frank was here.

April, Tuesday 1, 1873
I stayed at home all day and [at] nite went to the Burg. Lyme come here and stayed all nite.

April, Wednesday 2, 1873
I stayed at home all day. In the forenoon I walked on the road and in the afternoon stayed in the house. John and Lib and Sam and Early and Will Brewer was here. John and Lyme went to town. Lyme stayed all night.

April, Thursday 3, 1873
I stayed at home all day and at nite I went to the Burg.

April, Friday 4, 1873

I stayed at home all day and at nite I went to the Burg. Will Brewer was here and stayed all nite. Lafe [went] up to a party to Herbert's. Burr Soaper stole all the money - brown money container.

April, Saturday 5, 1873

I stayed at home all day and at nite I went to the Burg. It rained in the afternoon and the creek ran through the fields all over in the Flats. Max Hait was here and got 26 trout.

April, Sunday 6, 1873

I went down to Mr. Snell's and went to the Tole [Toll] House in the forenoon and in the afternoon Ed McConnell was here and Tim at night.

April, Monday 7, 1873

I stayed at home all day and drew manure and at nite I went to the Burg. Lyme and Tim was here.

April, Tuesday 8, 1873

I stayed at home all day and pitched over the hay. It got hot in the bottom. Father went to town at nite. I went to Smith's after 2 pigs. And then I went to Aunt Julia's [Beckwith] with Lyme and Het. They stayed all nite.

April, Wednesday 9, 1873

I worked on the road in the afternoon and in the forenoon pitched hay. Frank was here and Tim.

April, Thursday 10, 1873

I stayed at home all day. Father and Mother went to town. Frank Hill moved today. Frank and Lyme and Sarah McC was here. Lafe quit here today. I went to the Burg at nite.

April, Friday 11, 1873

I stayed at home all day and at nite up to Coe Owens to a dance. I got home about 3 o'clock.

Near the "Big Bridge" in Webbs Mills. Photograph taken in summer 2011.

April, Saturday 12, 1873
I stayed at home all day. It rained in the afternoon. I went to the Burg at nite. Mose Webb was here.

April, Sunday 13, 1873
I stayed at home all day. Lib and Sam and Early and Lyme and Jane and Alex. Frank Stofford come here to work. Sam stayed here to go to school.

April, Monday 14, 1873
I stayed at home in the forenoon and in the afternoon I helped Lyme move. He moved to Town. I drove the McCanns down and [drove] Tony back. I got home about 10 o'clock.

April, Tuesday 15, 1873
I stayed at home all day and at nite I went to the Burg.

April, Wednesday 16, 1873
I stayed at home all day. Father and Frank went up to Plank Road. Nat Hait was here and got a pheasant.

April, Thursday 17, 1873
I stayed at home all day and thrashed and shelled corn. Frank went to the Mill with a grist.

April, Friday 18, 1873
I stayed at home all day. Lyme and Sherm [Tanner] and Will [Helme] was here tonite. Lyme stayed all nite.

April, Saturday 19, 1873
I and Sam went up to John's and I went a-fishing. McCann was up and got the horses. We wacked all of the way. Lyme and Frank and father went to town. I stayed all nite up to John's. It rained most of the day.

April, Sunday 20, 1873
I went a-fishing and catched 8 trout. I stayed all night. Ed and Lyme and Mary and Jane and Ally [Alex?] Tony and Millie and Bertha and Frank come up here.

April, Monday 21, 1873
The snow is about 3 inches deep. I went a-hunting a little while. I killed a partridge.

April, Tuesday 22, 1873
I come home. Sam and ---. It snowed all day. Father went to town.

April, Wednesday 23, 1873
I stayed at home all day and at nite went to the Burg. There was a game to William Brace tonite.

April, Thursday 24, 1873
I stayed at home all day. I went down to the Burg after the mail and got the crowbar. I went to the store. Will Helme and Sherman Tanner was here to play Eucher.

April, Friday 25, 1873
I stayed at home all day. Ida Coe was here. Father and Frank went up to make Plank Road.

April, Saturday 26, 1873
I stayed at home all day. Lat Edison was here today. I went to the burg at nite.

April, Sunday 27, 1873
I stayed at home all day and at nite went to the meeing and to Jim's. Ed and his wife and son was here today. Tim was here.

April, Monday 28, 1873
I went down to Mr. Breese's and got his net to catch fish. We cleaned the fish pond. Father and Max Hait [Haight] and Cook and me we caught 9 trout. I went and took the net home.

April, Tuesday 29, 1873
I stayed at home all day. Father went to town. Frank and I went a-fishing at nite and we got a lot of fish. Mose Scofield had a vendue today. It rained all day.

April, Wednesday 30, 1873
I stayed at home all day. Father and I made a fence. I went to the Burg. Abbie Nicholds and Jim Brink was married today.

May, Thursday 1, 1873
I stayed at home all day and cut brush.

May, Friday 2, 1873
It rained. I went a-fishing and got a nice lot of fish. Father went to town.

May, Saturday 3, 1873
I went a-fishing. It rained all day.

May, Sunday 4, 1873
I stayed at home all day. John and Lib & Sam & Early & Elake Webster and Tim and Bill Patterson was here.

Seeley Creek was a good place to fish for trout in 1873.

May, Monday 5, 1873
I stayed at home all day and at nite I went to the Burg.

May, Tuesday 6, 1873
I stayed at home all day and made a fence around the school house. There was a dance up to James Carman's. There was five girls there. Father went to town.

May, Wednesday 7, 1873
I stayed at home all day and fixed fence and cut brush.

May, Thursday 8, 1873
I went down to the mill and at nite I went a-fishing. It rained all day.

May, Friday 9, 1873
I stayed here and made fence in the forenoon and in the afternoon I worked on the creek for Bradbury [Thomas Bradbury, farmer].

May, Saturday 10, 1873
I stayed at home all day. I went a-fishing at nite. Father went to town and Jane and Alex went up with him. Tim was here. Aunt Julia and Lib was here.

May, Sunday 11, 1873
I stayed at home all day. Dan was here.

May, Monday 12, 1873
I went to the burg in the forenoon and in the afternoon I stayed at home. Father went to town.

May, Tuesday 13, 1873
I stayed at home all day and at nite I went to the Burg. Het went to town today.

May, Wednesday 14, 1873

I stayed at home all day and at nite I went to the Burg. Father went to Botcher's today with Dan Beckwith. T. S. Judd was here today.

May, Thursday 15, 1873

I stayed at home all day. Frank got the oats all in today.

May, Friday 16, 1873

I stayed at home all day and at nite I went to the Burg and got some Brand. Father come home today. Harry Lyons was here today. Sam was home today.

May, Saturday 17, 1873

I stayed at home all day and at nite I went to the Burg.

May, Sunday 18, 1873

I went up home with Frank Stafford and we went a-fishing and we got 3 fish. Mary Harvey Lyons was here and Chris John [Christian] Watkins and Lib and Early & Sam come here.

May, Monday 19, 1873

I worked for Mr. Gosper on the big bridge & at nite Frank & I went a-fishing. We got 10 fish. Father and Mother went to town.

May, Tuesday 20, 1873

I stayed at home all day. Father went to town. I went a-fishing and got 8. Het and Sam went up to John's and stayed all nite.

May, Wednesday 21, 1873

I stayed at home all day and at nite I went to the burg and to the Temperance Lecture. Father went to town.

May, Thursday 22, 1873

I stayed at home all day and planted corn. Mr. Mosher helped us and at nite I went to the Burg and Sam and I went a-fishing. Mother went up to Miss Hill's.

May Sunday, 18 1873.

I went up home with
Frank Goffird and
we went a fishing
and we got 6 fish
Katy Harry Sam
was there and Cross
John Wadkins
and us and Early
Sam come home

May Monday, 19 1873.

I worked for Mr.
Jeffrey on the
Big Bridge &
at Wife Frank
and I went a shering
and we got 6
fish Father and
Mother went
to town

May, Friday 23, 1873
I went up on the Plank Road. We made 14 rods today.

May, Saturday 24, 1873
I stayed at home all day and at nite I went a-fishing.

May, Sunday 25, 1873
I went up to Lyme's. Lyme & Jane & Alex & Ed & Mary & Bailey and Tom & Bertha was here today. Elake and James at nite. I went to Ed's.

May, Monday 26, 1873
I stayed at home all day and plowed. Father and Frank went up and made Plank Road.

May, Tuesday 27, 1873
I stayed at home all day and plowed and at nite I went to the Burg. Frank quit today.

May, Wednesday 28, 1873
I stayed at home all day and at nite I went to the Burg.

May, Thursday 29, 1873
I went to town with a load of wood and got some plaster. And at nite I went to the Burg.

May, Friday 30, 1873
I went up to the Mill and a-sawed out planks and brot a load of Boards home.

May, Saturday 31, 1873
I stayed at home all day. Father and Het went to town.

June, Sunday 1, 1873
I went to Ed's and to James' in the afternoon. Ed & John and Lib and Early & Sam came here today to Sunday School. I went to the Consert to the Church.

June, Monday 2, 1873
I stayed to home all day. Father went to town and when he come back took a load of wood to town and went to the Burg.

June, Tuesday 3, 1873
I went up to make the Plank Road.

June, Wednesday 4, 1873
I went up to make the Plank Road and at nite I went to the Burg and to see the fishes to the Big Bridge. It rained here today.

June, Thursday 5, 1873
I worked on the Bridge for Mr. Gosper by Welles' house.

June, Friday 6, 1873
I stayed at home all day and at nite I went to the Burg.

June, Saturday 7, 1873
I stayed at home in the forenoon and in the afternoon I went to the shop with the horse. Father went to town. John come here today and Sam went home with him.

June, Sunday 8, 1873
I stayed at home all day and at nite I went down to Ed's and Mary Mapes had Meeting up to the schoolhouse today.

June, Monday 9, 1873
I went up to work on the Road.

June, Tuesday 10, 1873
I worked on the road up by the schoolhouse and at nite I went to Pine Woods [today's Pine City] and up to the store. It rained all day.

June, Wednesday 11, 1873
I worked on the road and at nite I went to the Burg and a-fishing and got about 50.

A current view of downtown Webbs Mills. Photograph taken in summer 2011.

June, Thursday 12, 1873

I stayed at home all day and made stump fence. Het went to town and brot Tony home with her.

June, Friday 13, 1873

I stayed at home all day and made stump fence and at nite went to the Burg.

June, Saturday 14, 1873

I went up to Mrs. Helme's and got corn shelled and hauled 8 bushels of corn in the forenoon and in the afternoon went a-fishing and I got a lot of fish. Father and Mother went to town today.

June, Sunday 15, 1873

I went up to John's and we went a-fishing and we got a lot of fish.

June, Monday 16, 1873

I drawed stone for Dr. Leonard in the forenoon and in the afternoon I made stump fence and at nite went to the Burg.

June, Tuesday 17, 1873

I stayed at home all day and made stump fence and at nite I went to the Burg. Mr. Bailey come here to work today.

June, Wednesday 18, 1873

I stayed at home all day and made stump fence and at nite I went to the Burg.

June, Thursday 19, 1873

I stayed at home all day and cultivated corn. Fet Miller worked here today. Em [Emma] Robbins come here today to sew.

June, Friday 20, 1873

I drawed stone to Dr. Leonard all day. Het Lockwood and Gusta Misner and Alex Schofield was here today. Ed McConnell come up here and I went to the Burg with him. John and Albert Robbins and Early come here and Sam went home with them.

June, Saturday 21, 1873

I stayed at home all day and howed corn. Father went to town and took Tom[?] home. At nite I went a-fishing down to Jim's and stayed all nite.

June, Sunday 22, 1873

I went a-fishing and got a lot of Bullheads.

June, Monday 23, 1873

In the forenoon went with a load of stones and got Mr. T--- T-- to top stumps and in the afternoon I made stump fence. Fet Miller was here today. At nite I went to the store.

June, Tuesday 24, 1873

In the forenoon went a-fishing and in the afternoon drawed stone to Tom Sheer.

June, Wednesday 25, 1873

I stayed at home all day and made stump fence.

June, Thursday 26, 1873

I drawed stone all day and at nite I went to the Burg. Het Miller was here today & Sarah McWhortle went to town and the horse run away with them and broke the wagon all to pieces and hurt them.

June, Friday 27, 1873

I stayed at home all day. Father went to town. Lanson White was here today.

June, Saturday 28, 1873

I stayed at home all day and at nite I went to the Burg. Mr. White was here and stayed all nite.

June, Sunday 29, 1873

In the morning Ed Scofield come here and we went up to Mr. Helme's and when I come home Lyme & Jane and Alex and Frank Cook and Ed and his wife and boy and John and Lib and Early and Miles McWhorter was here.

June, Monday 30, 1873

I stayed at home all day.

July, Tuesday 1, 1873
In the forenoon I made fence and in the afternoon I plowed up on the hill. At nite I went to the store and up to Dr. Leonard.

July, Wednesday 2, 1873
I stayed at home all day and at nite I went to the mill and got a load of Brand. Father bot all of the brand Mr. Brown had.

July, Thursday 3, 1873
I stayed at home in the forenoon and in the afternoon I went to the shop and got the horse shod and the wagon fixed. Father and John and Sam went to town. Mary Piper and her young ones was here today.

July, Friday 4, 1873
In the forenoon I drawed up brand and in the afternoon I went to town. I went over to Lyme and Ed's.

July, Saturday 5, 1873
I stayed at home all day. In the forenoon I drawed brand and in the afternoon I plowed and at nite I went to the Burg.

July, Sunday 6, 1873
I and Sam McWhorter went and got strawberries and in the afternoon I went down to Jim's and up to Ed's. Elake was here. Mr. Beckwith and his wife and sons come here and stayed all nite.

July, Monday 7, 1873
I stayed at home all day. Father went to town and Mr. Judd came home with him. Mr. White come here and stayed all nite.

July, Tuesday 8, 1873
I went to the mill and got a load of brand.

July, Wednesday 9, 1873
I stayed at home all day and planted corn and potatoes. Father went to town and took Mr. Judd.

A panorama of Webbs Mills. Photograph taken in summer 2011.

July, Thursday 10, 1873
I went up to Mr. Gosper's to a mowing bee in the morning and in the rest of the day I plowed.

July, Friday 11, 1873
I stayed at home all day and put in the buckwheat. Father went up to John's. At nite Same went home.

July, Saturday 12, 1873
I stayed at home all day. Father and Het went to town. Lib and Early and – Elison was here today.

July, Sunday 13, 1873
I stayed at home all day. Fet Miller and Ed McConnell was here and I went home with Ed.

July, Monday 14, 1873
In the forenoon I plowed for buckwheat and in the afternoon I went to the Mill and got a load of brand. Fet worked here today. Miny Barker come here today to work.

July, Tuesday 15, 1873
I went to the Mill and got a sack of flour. And then I went up to the mill and got a load of t---- and took to Mr. Edsell at Pine Woods. Fet worked here this afternoon. When I got home I got Mr. Wilder's jackscrews for to raise the barn.

July, Wednesday 16, 1873
I stayed at home all day and plowed corn. Fet walked here today. Father and Mother went to town and Tom come home with them.

July, Thursday 17, 1873
 I went to the Mill and got a load of brand. Fet worked here today.

July, Friday 18, 1873
I stayed at home all day and plowed corn. Fet worked here. Father went to town.

July, Saturday 19, 1873
I went to the Mill and got a load of brand and then helped raise the barn and at nite went to the Burg. Lafe Bailey come home with me and stayed all nite.

July, Sunday 20, 1873
I went a-berrying with Ed McConnell and Ed D--. We got about 19 quarts and at nite I went out a-walking.

July, Monday 21, 1873
I stayed at home all day and at nite I went and took Mr. Wilder jack screws home. Lyme come here today and stayed all nite. Jane Bentley was here.

July, Tuesday 22, 1873
I stayed at home all day. We begun haying today and at nite I went down to Pine Woods to a show.

July, Wednesday 23, 1873
I stayed at home all day. Father went to town. Lyme come here to day and him and Mother went up to John's. Lyme stayed all nite.

July, Thursday 24, 1873
I went to the shop and got the wagon wheel and then we drawed in hay. We finished up the orchard today and then we began to mow in the lot in front of the schoolhouse.

July, Friday 25, 1873
I stayed at home all day. I was sick. Lyme and Jane & Alex came here this morning and Lyme went to town after Mary and her to [two] girls. Tom was up here and Susan Colegrove and her three children. Lib and her to [two] children came here. They stayed all nite but Susie and to [two] of her children.

July, Saturday 26, 1873
 I stayed at home all day. I was sick. Mary and here three children was here and Susie and her three children and Lib and her two children and Lyme and Jane & Alex and Ed & Will Colegrove was here. Lib and Early and Lime & Jane & Alex went up to Cook's and all of the rest stayed all nite.

July, Sunday 27, 1873
The Company was here but Jane & Alex went up to John's and took Lib home and Tim went and took Ed's folks home.

July, Monday 28, 1873
I went down to the Burg to see if Ed would come and help us in haying. Lyme was here today. Miny [Minnie] come here to work today.

July, Tuesday 29, 1873
I stayed at home all day.

July, Wednesday 30, 1873
I stayed at home all day and at nite I went down to Ed's and stayed all nite.

July, Thursday 31, 1873
I stayed at home all day. Ed helped us today. Susie and Sarah was up here today.

August, Friday 1, 1873
I stayed at home all day and worked in the hay. Lyme and father went to town.

August, Saturday 2, 1873
I stayed at home all day and at nite I went to the store. Miny went home. -1-1-1.

August, Sunday 3, 1873
I went up to Lyme and got the wagon and then I went to Jim's and Ed's.

August, Monday 4, 1873
I stayed at home all day and at nite I went to the store. Ed & Steve Weaver helped us today and Bob Jenkins' father went to town. Mary and her children come here today.

August Friday, 8   1879.

it rained and all of the
men went home but
John Bil and george
Leney ch [?] &
george Matney
I went to the mill
in the Morning &
then I went to
Pine Woods to the
Sarah Ming Com
[?] and I went to
the stare at mill

August Saturday, 9   1879

I stayed at home all
day John and Bill
and george [?] of
no [?] went home
and I went to the
[?] Mary went home
—/ct—/

August, Tuesday 5, 1873
I stayed at home all day. Ed and Steve & George Teneyck & Bob and old Barnhart. He had his machine. Sarah and Frank, Mary and Nely [Nellie?] & Mary & Liby & Tang & Bertha & Aunt Julia and Liby was here today.

August, Wednesday 6, 1873
I stayed at home all day. John and Mary came over here today to work. All of the men help us but Bob and Barnhart.

August, Thursday 7, 1873
I stayed at home all day. All of the men helped us today and was an ice cream party at Lew Wells tonite. Sarah and Frank was here and stayed all nite. We went to the barn and slept [with?] all of the men.

August, Friday 8, 1873
It rained and all of the men went home buy John, Bill and George Teneyck helped & George Mosher and I went to the mill in the morning & and then went to Pine Woods to the shop. Miny come here to work. I went to the store at nite.

August, Saturday 9, 1873
I stayed at home all day. John and Bill and George helped us. John went home and I went to the Burg. Miny went home. --1-1-1.

August, Sunday 10, 1873
I went down to Ed's in the afternoon.

August, Monday 11, 1873
I stayed at home all day and cradled oats. George Mosher and George Teneyck helped me. Lyme and Jane and Alex was here. Mother went and took Mary & Liby & Tom & Bertha home today.

August, Tuesday 12, 1873
I stayed at home all day and cradled oats. Jessie Criss helped me today. George Teneyck helped me.

August, Wednesday 13, 1873
It rained all day. I went to the Mill and got a load of Brand.

August, Thursday 14, 1873
I went a-fishing. It rained all day.

August, Friday 15, 1873
I stayed at home all day and went a-berrying. Father went to town.

August, Saturday 16, 1873
I stayed at home all day and reaped oats & hay. Bill & George Teneyck & Bob and Jessie helped me today and at nite I went to the Burg.

August, Sunday 17, 1873
I went up to John's in the morning and then I went to town to meeting up to the lake. Mother and John & Lib & I.

August, Monday 18, 1873
I went to the Mill & got a load of brand. Lyme & Jane & Alex was here and stayed all nite. Susie and Jimy was here. George come here to work.

August, Tuesday 19, 1873
I drawed brand all day. Lyme was here.

August, Wednesday 20, 1873
I stayed at home all day and drew hay. Lyme was here. Father went to town today.

August, Thursday 21, 1873
I stayed at home all day and raked oats and at nite I went up to the schoolhouse to a show.

August, Friday 22, 1873
I stayed at home all day and drawed in oats. Jessie Criss helped me today.

August, Saturday 23, 1873
In the forenoon I mowed and drawed in oats and in the afternoon I went down to the Bulkhead to make a dam. And at nite I went to the Burg. Charley Baker was here today.

August, Sunday 24, 1873
I stayed at home all day and picked berries. Ed McConnell [was] here to work.

August, Monday 25, 1873
I went up to the dam and then I come home and went to town. Miny went with us to Ed's to work.

August, Tuesday 26, 1873
I went to work on the dam.

August, Wednesday 27, 1873
I went to the dam to work.

August, Thursday 28, 1873
I went to work on the dam.

August, Friday 29, 1873
I stayed at home all day and plowed in the forenoon and in the afternoon I finished drawing in the oats.

August, Saturday 30, 1873
I stayed at home all day. [some illegible writing] After g--- went to the shop twice. --- at nite went to the Burg. Father went to town. We had 45 loads.

August, Sunday 31, 1873
I stayed at home all day and at nite I went up to John's. Tim was here today. Sam come home with us.

September, Monday 1, 1873
I went to work on the dam. Bill Teneyck and David Morgan helped me in the afternoon. I came home and plowed.

September, Tuesday 2, 1873
I went down to work on the dam and then I come home and plowed.

September, Wednesday 3, 1873
I stayed at home all day and plowed.

September, Thursday 4, 1873
I stayed at home in the forenoon and in the afternoon I went to the mill and got a load of brand. We have got it all drawed up home.

September, Friday 5, 1873
I went to town and raised up Ed's house.

September, Saturday 6, 1873
I dragged for Dave in the forenoon and in the afternoon I went to the mill.

September, Sunday 7, 1873
I stayed at home all day. Ed and Lyme and Ed over to the dam. Father --- was here.

September, Monday 8, 1873
I went and worked on the road for Gosper with the team. Het went down to Lyme's.

September, Tuesday 9, 1873
In the forenoon I took Aunt Julia a load of wood and in the afternoon I plowed.

September, Wednesday 10, 1873
I stayed at home and plowed all day.

September, Thursday 11, 1873
I stayed at home all day. I finished plowing today. Father & Mother went to town. I dug potatoes this afternoon.

Seeley Creek. Photograph taken in summer 2011.

September, Friday 12, 1873
I stayed at home all day. Father went up to John's and got some wheat and this afternoon I dragged in wheat. I cut corn this forenoon.

September, Saturday 13, 1873
I stayed at home all day & dragged in wheat. I got done and at nite I went to the store. Het come home to nite.

September, Sunday 14, 1873
I stayed at home all day. Father & Mother went up to John's. I went up to Ed's at nite.

September, Monday 15, 1873
I stayed at home all day & cut corn. Father went to town.

September, Tuesday 16, 1873
I stayed at home all day. Finished a-cutting corn. Went up to John's at nite and got John's folks to go to the show.

September, Wednesday 17, 1873
I went to the show and then went and took John's folks home & stayed all nite.

September, Thursday 18, 1873
I went to the show and the rest of the time I stayed at home.

September, Friday 19, 1873
I stayed at home all day and dragged & aggravated in rye. I got done. Lafe was here & stayed all nite.

September, Saturday 20, 1873
I went up to John's and dragged his fallow over. When we was a-going up we ran against another wagon and Father fell out and hurt him[self]. I stayed all nite and we went a-cooning.

September, Sunday 21, 1873
I went with John and we cut a stick and made a drag and then I come home. Ed & Lyme and Ed McConnell and Elake and the boys and Liby was here. Tim was here.

September, Monday 22, 1873
I went down to Dave's and got our cradle and then cradled buckwheat and this afternoon I burnt at the meadows and at nite I went to the store.

September, Tuesday 23, 1873
I went and took our young cattle up to Hiram Redstick [Hiram Redfield?] And then I went to the mill this afternoon. I helped bay [bay horse] out a-trotting on Bill Mapes' land.

September, Wednesday 24, 1873
I stayed at home all day and cradled buckwheat and at nite I went down to Dave's to an apple cut. Daniel Gray was buried today.

September, Thursday 25, 1873
This forenoon I went and cut some sticks for a log rigging and this afternoon I went to the shop.

September, Friday 26, 1873
I stayed at home this forenoon and this afternoon I went up and got a load of logs up to John's. Lyme and L-- was here and stayed all nite. Sam come home with me.

This barn is probably not the Marvin's barn, but it is currently on the former Marvin property. Photograph taken in summer 2011.

| SEPT. | SATURDAY, 27 | 1879. | SEPT. | SUNDAY, 28 | 1879. |

Stayed at home all day and mowed Buckwheat and then I drawed in potatoes and of nite I went to the store and up to Steves moved.

in the morning I went and got some Chestnuts and in the afternoon I went a hunting Ed McConnell & Bill Kirbarn and his wife & Jim & Jane Kirby & Jahn and Lyf & Carly was here they went home Jim Jane went home

September, Saturday 27, 1873
I stayed at home all day and mowed buckwheat and then drawed in potatoes and at nite I went to the store and up to Steve Weaver's.

September, Sunday 28, 1873
In the morning I went and got some Chestnuts and in the afternoon I went a-hunting. Ed McConnell & Bill McCann and his wife & Lyme & Dan Mack & John and Lib & Early was here. Het went home with Lyme. Sam went home.

September, Monday 29, 1873
I stayed at home all day and worked on the road.

September, Tuesday 30, 1873
I stayed at home all day and worked on the road.

October, Wednesday 1, 1873
I drawed logs for John. I made 3 trips and broke my wagon.

October, Thursday 2, 1873
I stayed at home all day and raked buckwheat and gathered chestnuts.

October, Friday 3, 1873
I drawed logs & thrashed buckwheat. Het come home.

October, Saturday 4, 1873
I drawed logs & made fence and then went down to the shop. I went up to Ed's and found Mart there. I stayed all nite.

October, Sunday 5, 1873
When I come home Ed & Mart and Jim came home with me and then I went down to Jim's to dinner and then I came home and milked and then I went down to Ed's. Mart came home with me and stayed all nite.

October, Monday 6, 1873
I stayed at home all day. Ed was here. I went to Ed's and stayed all nite.

October, Tuesday 7, 1873
It snowed so that I did not get home till almost noon and this afternoon I picked apples and chestnuts. Father went to town. Mother went down to Aunt Julia's and stayed all nite.

October, Wednesday 8, 1873
I stayed at home all day and raked and thrashed buckwheat. Mart was here and stayed all nite. Bob and Hiram & Jessie helped thrash. I and Mart went up to John Ray's to a spree at nite.

October, Thursday 9, 1873
I stayed at home all day and thrashed buckwheat and at nite went to the Burg.

October, Friday 10, 1873
I stayed at home all day and thrashed buckwheat and at nite I went down to Wilson Mashel's [Michael's?] to a dance.

October, Saturday 11, 1873
I stayed at home all day. I drawed stone in the forenoon and in the afternoon I plowed and dragged in rye and at nite I went to the store.

October, Sunday 12, 1873
I stayed at home all day. Lyme & Frank was here.

October, Monday 13, 1873
I went and took a load of brush to Wells [Lewis Wells] and then I picked stones. Hait is sick.

October, Tuesday 14, 1873
In the forenoon I drawed soad [sowed] corn and in the afternoon I went to town and at nite I went to [the] school meeting.

October, Wednesday 15, 1873
I drawed logs all day. Tim & Mr. White & Mrs. Cole & Miny was here. -1-1-1

October, Thursday 16, 1873
I work on the dam. Bill Teneyck & Jim St. Clare helped today.

October, Friday 17, 1873
I drawed logs all day. Frank & Bill & Jim worked in the afternoon.

October, Saturday 18, 1873
I picked apples all day. At nite I went up to John's to help them cut a big tree. I stayed all nite. Jane and Alex was here.

October, Sunday 19, 1873
I came home from John's. Jane and Alex and Lyme & Frank and Ed & Mary & Bertha was here.

October, Monday 20, 1873
I stayed at home all day and cleaned up buckwheat. It rained all day. It snowed about one inch last nite.

October, Tuesday 21, 1873
I stayed at home all day and picked apples.

October, Wednesday 22, 1873
I stayed at home all day and picked apples. Net Humel came here to work today.

October, Thursday 23, 1873
I stayed at home all day and drawed gravel and corn. Sarah McWhorter was here. Lyme was here. I went to the shop at nite.

October, Friday 24, 1873
In the forenoon I went to the shop and in the after[noon] I made sider [cider]. O.H. Fitch and two of his girls and Mr. T--- and his wife and girl & Lyme was here.

October, Saturday 25, 1873
I stayed at home all day and husked corn and at nite I went to the store. Father went to town. Lib and Early was here and stayed all nite.

October, Sunday 26, 1873
I stayed at home all day. Ed McConnell was here - we went a-hunting a little while. We got a rabbit.

October, Monday 27, 1873
I made cider in the forenoon and in the afternoon husked corn.

October, Tuesday 28, 1873
I went to the shop in the morning and then I husked corn.

October, Wednesday 29, 1873
I went after the Doctor for Father and then I husked corn. Elake was here. It snowed most of the day.

October, Thursday 30, 1873
I stayed at home all day and husked corn and at nite I went up to George Mosher's and took Covel's horse up there.

October, Friday 31, 1873
I stayed at home all day and husked corn. We got all of the corn husked that was in the field. There is some in the barn.

November, Saturday 1, 1873
I went to town with Father. I went to Ed's and to Lyme's. I got me a new suit of close [clothes].

November, Sunday 2, 1873
I went a-hunting in the forenoon and in the afternoon I went up to George's with Lyme. I come down as far as the Tanner's and then I went back to [the] meeting up to the schoolhouse.

November, Monday 3, 1873
I stayed at home all day and husked oats. Father went to town. At nite I went to the store.

NOVEMBER TUESDAY, 4 1879.

I stayed at home all day and about [pumpkins?] and [?] I went out to [?] and took [?] [?] [?] to [?] went to Election

NOVEMBER WEDNESDAY, 5 1879.

I stayed at home all day and [?] [?] Father went to [?] Went to the [?] at nite

November, Tuesday 4, 1873
I stayed at home all day and drawed pumpkins and at nite I went up to John's and took him home. Father went to Election.

November, Wednesday 5, 1873
I stayed at home all day and picked stone. Father went to town. I went to the Burg at nite.

November, Thursday 6, 1873
I stayed at home all day and drawed manure. Father went down to Aunt Julia's.

November, Friday 7, 1873
I stayed at home all day and drawed manure and plowed and picked stone. Father went up to Wells' to work on the dam.

November, Saturday 8, 1873
I stayed at home all day and drawed stone and at nite I went to the store. I went to the store. Father worked on the dam.

November, Sunday 9, 1873
I stayed at home all day. Ed was here.

November, Monday 10, 1873
I stayed at home all day and drawed manure and corn stalks. Petey was here to work.

November, Tuesday 11, 1873
I stayed at home all day and drawed manure and corn stalks. At nite I went to John's to work.

November, Wednesday 12, 1873
I stayed here all day and cut logs. Mr. Robbins helped me.

November, Thursday 13, 1873
I stayed here and sawed logs. Mr. Robbins helped me.

November, Friday 14, 1873
I stayed here and sawed logs all day. John helped me.

November, Saturday 15, 1873
I worked half a day and in the afternoon I went home and got the gun. John went to Waverly.

November, Sunday 16, 1873
I went a-hunting. I killed nothing.

November, Monday 17, 1873
I stayed here and made a r--d and drawed out wood.

November, Tuesday 18, 1873
I stayed here all day and cut wood and husked corn in the forenoon and in the afternoon I went a-hunting. John come to nite.

November, Wednesday 19, 1873
I come home to day and this afternoon I cut logs and wood.

November, Thursday 20, 1873
I stayed at home all day and cut logs and wood.

November, Friday 21, 1873
I stayed at home all day and cut wood and logs.

November, Saturday 22, 1873
I stayed at home all day and cut wood and at nite I went to the store and and up to Elake's. Ed come up home and stayed all nite. His wife has gone up home. Susie and Jim went with her.

November, Sunday 23, 1873
I stayed at home all day. I went a-hunting a little while at nite. I went down home with Ed.

November, Monday 24, 1873
School commenced today. Our teacher's name is Pild. I went to the store at nite and Ed come home with me. He stayed all nite.

November, Tuesday 25, 1873
I went to school. Ed worked here today. Father went to town.

November, Wednesday 26, 1873
I went to school. Peter drawed logs.

November, Thursday 27, 1873
I stayed at home all day and cut logs.

November, Friday 28, 1873
I went to school. At nite I went to the Burg. Later went up to John's.

November, Saturday 29, 1873
I stayed at home all day and cut logs in the forenoon. I went a-hunting. I killed a partridge. Jessie & Bill Criss come here and helped kill a bull.

November, Sunday 30, 1873
I went a-hunting with Peter and Father. Father killed a partridge.

December, Monday 1, 1873
I went to school. It snowed all day.

December, Tuesday 2, 1873
I went to school. I took a load of wood to Aunt Julia's. Lyme was here and stayed all nite.

December, Wednesday 3, 1873
I went to school. Lyme was here and worked a half day. I went a-hunting a little while at nite.

December, Thursday 4, 1873
I went to school. Peter drawed wood and stone.

December, Friday 5, 1873
I went to school. Lyme was here got a load of stone. I went to the Burg at nite.

December, Saturday 6, 1873
I stayed at home all day and cut wood. Father and Mother went to town. I went to the Burg at nite.

December, Sunday 7, 1873
I went a-hunting a little while. We got a rabbit. Tim was here. I went a-skating a little while.

December, Monday 8, 1873
I went to school. Father went to town.

December, Tuesday 9, 1873
I went to school. Father went to town.

December, Wednesday 10, 1873
I went to school and at nite I went up to the schoolhouse to a spelling school. Lyme and Charlie Pierce was here and stayed all nite.

December, Thursday 11, 1873
I went to school. Lyme and Charlie worked here all day.

December, Friday 12, 1873
I went to school all day and at nite I went to the Burg. Father went to town. Peter quit work here today.

December, Saturday 13, 1873
I drawed lumber all day. I drawed three loads home from the mill and two up to U.B Dann

December, Sunday 14, 1873
I stayed at home all day and at nite I went to Ed's and stayed a little while.

December, Monday 15, 1873
I went to school all day. The teacher offered a present to the [student] who would have the most credits.

DECEMBER WEDNESDAY, 24 1879.

I went to school
all day and at
nite I went to the
Burg

DECEMBER THURSDAY, 25 1879.

in the fore noon
I went a hunting
and in the after noon
I cut logs
John and Lieb
and Sam & Early
& [illegible]
& [illegible] together
at nite I went
up to Johns
to a dance

December, Tuesday 16, 1873
I went to school all day and then at nite I went up to spelling school.

December, Wednesday 17, 1873
I went to school all day. Miss Hill and Miss Huntley was here today.

December, Thursday 18, 1873
I went to school all day.

December, Friday 19, 1873
I went to school all day.

December, Saturday 20, 1873
In the forenoon I drawed wood and in the afternoon I cut wood. Father went to town. He took Covel's horse home.

December, Sunday 21, 1873
I went a-hunting. I got a rabbit. In the afternoon I went to the store ------- a fine time alone.

December, Monday 22, 1873
I went to school all day.

December, Tuesday 23, 1873
I went to school all day and at nite I went up to the schoolhouse to spelling school. Lafe Bailey come here to work to nite.

December, Wednesday 24, 1873
I went to school all day and at nite I went to the Burg.

December, Thursday 25, 1873
In the forenoon I went a-hunting and in the afternoon I cut logs. John and Lib and Sam & Early & Aunt Julia & Libbie was here. At nite I went up to John's to a dance.

December, Friday 26, 1873
I went to school all day. Lafe drawed out headin for M.B. Dann or [U.B.?]

December, Saturday 27, 1873
I and Lafe went over to John's --- and took Frank Hall's cow[?] home. We went a-horse back.

December, Sunday 28, 1873
I stayed at home all day and at nite Lafe and I went a-riding. Lyme and Jane was here and stayed all nite.

December, Monday 29, 1873
I went to school all day. Lafe drawed logs. Father went to town. Lyme and Charley was here and stayed all nite. I went to the store at nite.

December, Tuesday 30, 1873
I went to school all day. I went up to Criss's and got a big kettle for to kill hogs. I went down to Dave's and helped kill turkeys.

December, Wednesday 31, 1873
I stayed at home all day and killed hogs. Lyme and Charley and Bill Teneyck helped us. I went to the store at nite.

January, Thursday 1, 1874
Stayed at home all day and all ---. Lyme and Charley was here.

January, Friday 2, 1874
I went to school all day. The teacher kept me after school to learn a piece and at nite I went to the school to spelling school.

January, Saturday 3, 1874
I went with Lafe over to U.B. Dams with a load of ----- and then I helped draw wood. Father went to town. We went to the Burg at nite.

January, Sunday 4, 1874
I went up to Nate Brewer's with Lafe. It is more that a Hundred miles up there. [But somehow he seems to makes it back to school the next day?]

January, Monday 5, 1874
I went to school all day. Lafe plowed all day.

January, Tuesday 6, 1874
I went to school all day. Lafe plowed. I went to the Burg at nite. Carrie Nichols died last nite.

January, Wednesday 7, 1874
In the forenoon I helped clean up some wheat and in the afternoon. I went to Carrie Nichols' funeral. I went for a [pall] bearer.

January, Thursday 8, 1874
I went to school all day. Lafe plowed all day. I went up to Pa Tanner at nite. Lyme come up here to plow.

January, Friday 9, 1874
I went to school all day. Lafe went off today and did not work.

January, Saturday 10, 1874
I stayed at home all day and pulled stumps and drawed stone. Lyme went home. I went to the store at nite.

January, Sunday 11, 1874
I stayed at home all day. Lyme come up here to work.

January, Monday 12, 1874
I went to school all day. Lyme was here and drawed wood off from the hill. At nite I went to Sam Miller's and took Het up there.

January, Tuesday 13, 1874
I went to school all day. Lyme went up to the mill and got a load of wood and took it home and then he come back and stayed all nite. I went up to spelling school at nite. She had a large crowd – the most there to nite that there ever was.

January, Wednesday 14, 1874
I went to school all day. Lyme was here and worked for Mr. Stowell.

A view from today's Big Bridge looking toward Webbs Mills. Photograph taken summer 2011.

January, Thursday 15, 1874
I went to school all day and at nite I went to the Post office and to the Burg.

January, Friday 16, 1874
I went to school all day and at night I went up to Harris Jenkins' to a dance. There was one up to M-- Haven's and one to Pine Woods Hotel.

January, Saturday 17, 1874
I went to Aunt Julia's with a load of wood and when I come home I went to the mill and got a load of hulls and this afternoon I got a load of hulls and then I went up to Sam Miller's and got Het and at nite I went to the store. Nettie Hurnel[?] was here today.

January, Sunday 18, 1874
I stayed at home all [day] and done nothing. Father and Mother went up to John's and Sam come home with them. Het is sick. Tim was here.

January, Monday 19, 1874
I went to school all day. Sam went to school. Father went to town.

JANUARY SATURDAY, 18 1879.

I went to Aunt Julias
with a load of Wood
and when I come
home I went to the
mill and got a load
of hulls and this after
noon I got 2 load
of Hulls and then
I went up to
Sam Millers and
got Het and at
nite I went to
the Store
Nettie Hummel
was here today

JANUARY SUNDAY, 19 1879.

I stayed at House
and done
Nothing Father
and Mother
went up to Johns
and Sara come
home with
them Obet is
sick
Jim was Here

January, Tuesday 20, 1874
I went to school all day and at nite I went up to the schoolhouse to spelling school.
-1-1-1 S.M. Ed Barnhart come here to work.

January, Wednesday 21, 1874
I went to school all day and at nite I went up to Brown's schoolhouse to meeting and when we come back we stayed on the Road.

January, Thursday 22, 1874
I went to school all day and at nite I went to the Post office.

January, Friday 23, 1874
I went to school all day and at nite I went out to scallahoot. There was a sociable to Mr. Weeks'.

January, Saturday 24, 1874
I stayed home all day and cut logs. Ed went home. Lyme & Frank was here and stayed all nite. Lafe was here & stayed all nite. I went to the Burg at nite. There was a concert to the Church & there was not enough to pay and so they sojourned it until Monday night.

January Sunday 25, 1874
I stayed at home all day. Lyme & Frank stayed all day. Ed McConnell was here. There was meeting up to the schoolhouse today. Father & Sam went.

January Monday 26, 1874
I went to school all day & at night I went down to the Post office & then I come home and then I went down to the concert at the church.

January Tuesday 27, 1874
I went to school all day and at nite I went up to spelling school. We had a house full tonight. Mathis Knapp and Eliza & Lifa Miller was here and stayed till 12 o'clock. I got through my Arithmetic today.

January, Wednesday 28, 1874
I went to school all day. Ed drawed stone this afternoon. This forenoon he drawed logs.

January, Thursday 29, 1874
I went to school all day and at nite I went to the Post office and up to the store. Ed went home today at noon.

January Friday 30, 1874
I went up and helped clean the schoolhouse. It took all day. At nite I went to the shoe shop.

January, Saturday 31, 1874
I stayed home all day and cut logs and at nite I went to the store.

February, Sunday 1, 1874
I stayed at home all day. John and Lib Flynn and Early & John Kile was here & Bell Patterson was here. Tim was here.

February, Monday 2, 1874
I went to school all day and at nite went to bed as usual. I killed Dave McWhorter's dog. He was up here last night killing sheep.

February, Tuesday 3, 1874
I went to school all day and at nite I went to spelling school and up to Helme's to a sociable and stayed a little while and come home. There was about 20 there.

February, Wednesday 4, 1874
I went to school all day and at nite I went down and helped Ed unload a load of bark & then went to the Burg. Sam went home today.

February, Thursday 5, 1874
I went to school all day and at nite I went to the store. There was a donation to Abe Breese's house tonite.

February Friday, 6 1879.

I went to school all day and at nite I went to the Burg

Henry Marvin
Webbs Mills
Chemung Co.
N.Y.

February Saturday, 7 1879.

I stayed at home in the Forenoon and cut logs and in the afternoon I went down and helped Ed onload a load Bark and then we come Back and went up to Tanners and got a load of wood and took it down to aunt Sylvias and at nite I went up to Sam Millers to a Dance I got home at one o'clock

February, Friday 6, 1874
I went to school all day and at nite I went to the Burg.
Henry Marvin
Webbs Mills,
Chemung County

February, Saturday 7, 1874
I stayed at home in the forenoon and cut logs and in the afternoon I went down and helped Ed unload a load of bark and then we come back and went up to Tanner's and got a load of wood and took it down to Aunt Julia's and at nite I went up to Sam Miller's to a dance. I got home at one o'clock.

February, Sunday 8, 1874
I stayed at home all day and at nite I went down to Ed McConnell's. Charley Pierce come here to work.

February, Monday 9, 1874
I went to school all day and at nite I went to the Burg.

February Tuesday 10, 1874
I went to school all day and at nite I went up to the schoolhouse to spelling school. They stabbed it at me like God sake. Father discharged Charley today. Bill Miller come here tonite to work.

February Wednesday 11, 1874
I went to school all day and at nite I went to the store.

February, Thursday 12, 1874
I went to school all day and at nite I went up to the schoolhouse to a lecture.

February, Friday 13, 1874
I went to school all day and at nite we had a Dance here. There was about 50 here. I went up and got Sarah Manroe. She stayed all nite.

February, Saturday 14, 1874

I stayed at home all day and at nite I went up to the schoolhouse to a spelling school. Sarah went home tonite 1-1-1- Lyme was here and stayed all nite.

February, Sunday 15, 1874

I went to town and got Jane and Alex and the baby. Tim was here.

February Wednesday 16, 1874

I went to school all day and at night I went to the Burg.

February, Thursday 17, 1874

I went to school all day, and at nite I went up to the schoolhouse to spelling school. I come home. There was not many there to nite. Ed come here to work today.

End of Diary

Hebrews 11:4
"By faith Abel offered unto God a more excellent sacrifice than Cain, by which he obtained witness that he was righteous, God testifying of his gifts: and by it he being dead yet speaketh."

written in the back of Henry's diary

A packet of reddish-brown hair was in the back pocket of Henry's diary.

The Marvin-Beckwith Cemetery is just north of Beckwith Road on Pennsylvania Avenue in Pine City, New York. Henry is supposedly buried there, but our research team was unable to find his stone. Photograph taken in summer 2011.

Afterward

Henry did not marry. He died on April 8, 1890 and is supposedly buried in the Marvin/Beckwith Cemetery in Pine City, although his stone is not visible. Henry's nephew, Ross Marvin, by brother Edward [sometimes Edwin], was the famous Arctic explorer with the Peary expedition who was murdered at the North Pole in 1909.

Henry also had a famous great-grand-nephew through his brother Edward's son Henry. Henry's son was Lamont Marvin, who fathered Hollywood actor Lee Marvin.

> *Fall from a steamer's burning deck,*
> *Fall from a housetop and break your neck,*
> *Fall from the starry Heavens above,*
> *But for God's sake, don't fall in love.*

written in the back of Henry's diary

Marvin Family History

From Ausburn Towner, "Our County and its People: A History of the Valley and County of Chemung..." (Syracuse, NY, 1892), pp. 45-46:

> *"In the year 1786 Gen. James Clinton, Gen. John Hathorn, and John Cantine, esq., were appointed commissioners on the part of the State of New York to survey the lands in the Chemung region....He[Gen. Hathorn] came into Orange County from Wilmington, Del., where he was born in 1749....Betsey Elizabeth, a daughter of Gen. John Hathorn, married Archibald Marvin, whose father, Gen. Seth Marvin, was with the commissioners in their survey of the county in 1788, and who purchased a large tract of land in Southport....Archibald Marvin had a son also named Seth, a noted man and prominent farmer living 'up the plank road' in Southport. Mrs. Archibald Marvin was one of the loveliest of women in person and character. As a widow for many years she lived with her daughter, Mrs. Julia Beckwith, in the locality named."]*

From "Descendants of Thomas Merveyn Mervyn:"

Archibald [Marvin] married Elizabeth Betsey Hathorne. Elizabeth was born on 27 Apr 1781 in Warwick, NY. She died on 2 Jul 1857. She was buried in Marvin/Beckwith Cemetery, Southport, Chemung, NY.

They had the following children:
Hector C Marvin was born on 5 Nov 1801. He died on 1 March 1874. He was buried in Marvin/Beckwith Cemetery, Southport, Chemung, NY.
Welling Marvin was born on 11 Dec 1803. He died on 9 Sep 1844. He was buried in Marvin/Beckwith Cemetery, Southport, Chemung, NY.
Decoe Marvin
Anthony Marvin
Seth Marvin
Mark Marvin was born on 4 Aug 1812. He died on 23 Nov 1824. He was buried in Marvin/Beckwith Cemetery, Southport, Chemung, NY.
Julia Ann Marvin (Beckwith)

Seth Marvin (descended from Archibald Marvin, Seth Marvin, Elihu Marvin, John Marvin, Matthew Marvin, Matthew Marvin, Edward A. Mervyn Marvin, Reinold Rynalde Marven, John, Thomas Merveyn) was born on 13 Jul 1810 in New York. He died on 9 Jun 1890 in Chemung, NY. He was buried in Marvin/Beckwith Cemetery, Southport, Chemung, NY.

Seth married (first wife) Lydia in 1835. Lydia was born in 1812. She died on 8 Jun 1838. She was buried in Marvin/Beckwith Cemetery, Southport, Chemung, NY.

They had the following children:
Edward Marvin
Sarah L. Marvin was born on 20 Jan 1838 in Southport, Chemung, New York. She died on 2 Jul 1839. She was buried in Marvin/Beckwith Cemetery, Southport, Chemung, NY.

Seth married (second wife) Matilda Jane McConnell in 1839. Matilda was born on 23 Oct 1820 in New York. She died on 26 Feb 1888. She was buried in Marvin/Beckwith Cemetery, Southport, Chemung, NY.

They had the following children:
Elizabeth Marvin was born in 1839 in Southport, Chemung, New York.
Lyman Marvin was born in 1842 in Southport, Chemung, New York.
Lawrence Marvin was born on 15 Sep 1845 in Southport, Chemung, New York. He died on 20 Jan 1846.
Emma Marvin was born on 12 Jul 1848 in Southport, Chemung, New York. She died on 12 Jul 1859. She was buried in Marvin/Beckwith Cemetery, Southport, Chemung, NY.
Adeline [Addie] Marvin was born on 28 Oct 1849 in Southport, Chemung, New York. She died on 14 Oct 1864. She was buried in Marvin/Beckwith Cemetery, Southport, Chemung, NY.
Helen Marvin was born in 1852 in Southport, Chemung, New York.
Henry Marvin was born on 14 Feb 1855 in Webbs Mills, Chemung, New York. He died on 8 Apr 1890.

Bibliography

Elmira *Telegram*, Sunday November 12, 1893 "Death of John Hathorn"

Elmira *Daily Gazette and Free Press* March 7, 1898 page 5 "Plank Road Question"

Descendants of Thomas Merveyn Mervyn http://home.gci.net/~themarvins/LSM/gen/web/MARVIN/21May2005/pafg69.htm#21127

Towner, Ausburn. *Our county and its people: a history of the valley and county of Chemung, from the closing years of the eighteenth century.* Syracuse, New York: D. Mason & Co., 1892.

More *Learning From History* publications from
New York History Review Press

A Darned Good Time
by Miss Lucy Potter, 1868

*My Centennial Diary - A Year in the Life of a
Country Boy* by Earll K. Gurnee, 1876

My Story - A Year in the Life of a Country Girl
by Ida Burnett, 1880

Queen City Adventure
by Emma Latier, 1902

Home In These Hills
by Viola Coolbaugh, 1891

www.ingramcontent.com/pod-product-compliance
Ingram Content Group UK Ltd.
Pitfield, Milton Keynes, MK11 3LW, UK
UKHW041958230426
12048UKWH00008B/412